Welcome to World of Drums.

A Drum kit is a **serious** but **fun** instrument to learn, and with time you will discover many different styles of playing, from **CLASSICAL** to **MODERN** & **ROCK**.
But all of this takes time!

We want to make sure that you do the right training at home and take on the challenge. So, just like top athletes in all different sports you too can compete and play at the **top level!**

THE CHALLENGE IS ON!

REMEMBER
1. If you do not understand anything, ask your coach. (Teacher).
2. Make sure you do **10 minutes** Home Training every day.
3. Get your parents to sign your training schedule, because the points you get all go towards your final awards.
4. Sometimes Home Training is hard but NEVER let it beat you!

STICK AT IT, WORK HARD, HAVE FUN, YOU WILL BE THE BEST!!!

©2008 by Southern Counties Music Services Limited. Photocopying is illegal.

Home Training Schedule

NAME: Joe

TERM: ....

HOME TRAINING SIGNATURES & CLASS POINTS

▼ PARENTS PLEASE INITIAL TO ACKNOWLEDGE 10 MINUTE TRAINING SESSION EACH DAY.

Day:	1	2	3	4	5	6	7	WEEKLY WORKOUT	TRAINING ZONE	BRAIN TEASER	TOTALS	BONUS
week 1:	SB	SB			SB	SB	SB	1	1	1	3	3
week 2:	SB	SB		SB	SB	SB	SB	1	1	1	9	3
week 3:	SB	SB	SB		SB		SB	1	1	1	8	2
week 4:	SB	SB	SB	SB			SB	5	1	1	7	2
week 5:	SB	SB	SB	SB			SB	5	1	1	7	2
week 6:				SB		SB		2	1	1	4	1
week 7:		SB	SB	SB		SB	SB	5	1	1	7	2
week 8:	SB	SB		SB		SB	SB	5	1	1	7	2
week 9:		SB		SB		SB	SB	4	1	1	6	1
week 10:	SB	SB		SB		SB		4	1	1	6	1
								GRAND TOTAL (MAX 100)			69	18
								GRAND TOTAL INC. BONUSES				87

▶ COACH ADD YOUR MARKS HERE

This Training Schedule is for you to **earn points by practising.** You will get a maximum of 7 points for a successful week's training and your teacher will give you an **extra point** for each section that you've completed. You may also earn **bonus points** for good work or for trying very hard.

END OF TERM AWARDS

END OF COURSE TOTALS:	65 POINTS	PASS	BRONZE
	75 POINTS	MERIT	SILVER
	85 POINTS	DISTINCTION	GOLD

©2008 by Southern Counties Music Services Limited. Photocopying is illegal.

Junior Drum Trainer™ BASICS

THE DRUM KIT

Parts of the drum kit.

- Ride cymbal
- Medium tom
- High tom
- Crash cymbal
- High hat open
- Floor tom
- Snare drum
- Bass (kick) drum
- Draw your own logo here!

Music basics.

The TIME SIGNATURE

DRUM CLEF   MUSICAL STAVE

MUSIC lives on the **MUSICAL STAVE**.
It is made up of **5 LINES & 4 SPACES**.

SCAMPS On-line.
You'll find **tips**, **help files** and **animated demonstrations** to help you through this book on our website - www.scampsmusic.com. **See you there soon!**

www.scampsmusic.com

©2008 by Southern Counties Music Services Limited. Photocopying is illegal.

Junior Drum Trainer™ WEEK: 1

WEEKLY WORKOUT

Get a grip.

This is the correct way to hold the drumsticks. They are held between the **flat of the thumb** and the **2nd joint of the index finger** (the fulcrum).

The rest of the fingers wrap around the stick loosely.

Notice the gap between the thumb and index finger.

NEVER close the gap. If you do the sticks won't bounce.

TRAINING ZONE

Your first drum roll.

Rolls are used in all types of drumming. This week we will learn to play a **single stroke roll** on the **snare drum**.

Set the metronome to ♩ = 120

This sign means repeat.

On the CD you will hear the roll played at the speed of **120 quarter beats per minute (BPM)**. Start at that tempo, then gradually increase the speed until you can play it at **200bpm or faster.**

IMPORTANT NOTES: Practice slowly. Don't pull back before the stroke. Let the sticks bounce. Use your wrists and not your arms.

BRAIN TEASER

Drum Notation.

1. Kick drum
2. Floor tom
3. Snare drum
4. Medium tom
5. High tom
6. Ride cymbal
7. High hat closed
8. High hat open
9. Crash cymbal

Unlike other musical instruments, drums do not have musical pitches. The drum kit has its own special kind of notation.

MEMORY PRACTICE: Memorise the names of the drums and where they sit on the musical stave. We will be having a note race soon.

So get training!!!

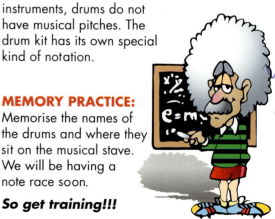

Junior Drum Trainer™ WEEK:2

WEEKLY WORKOUT

Double stroke roll day.

Set the metronome to ♩ = 120

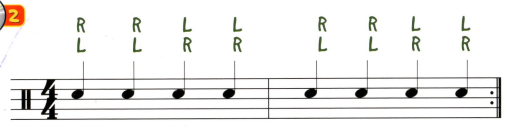

Today we will be looking at the **DOUBLE STROKE ROLL.**
This is simply two bounces with each hand. **R R L L R R L L R R L L R R L L** etc.
The nickname is the **'Mummy - Daddy' Roll**.
If you are right handed start with the right hand. If you are left handed start with the left hand.

TRAINING ZONE

New rudiment - the paradiddle.

Rudiments are rhythm and beat exercises for drummers. Throughout the course we will be looking at various different rudiments. The **paradiddle** is a combination of single and double strokes. A lot of drummers use this exercise on the kit. For fun see how many times you can say **paradiddle** in **10 seconds**.

Set the metronome to ♩ = 120 **Week 1:** [   ] Times   **Week 2:** [   ] Times

BRAIN TEASER

Type of notes.

Notes		Beats		Rests
𝅝	WHOLE	= 4	=	▬
𝅗𝅥	HALF	= 2	=	▬
♩	QUARTER	= 1	=	𝄽
♪	EIGHTH	= ½	=	𝄾

Here are most of the different types of **notes** and **rests** used in music - each one lasts for a different number of **beats**.

Try to **memorise** all the names and how long they are - you'll be using them soon!

©2008 by Southern Counties Music Services Limited. Photocopying is illegal.

Junior Drum Trainer™ WEEK:3

WEEKLY WORKOUT

Your first "Rock" beat.

Today we are going to look at a basic 'Rock' beat.

Start with just the hi hat.

Set the metronome to ♩ = 100

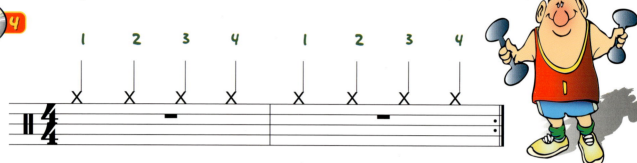

TRAINING ZONE

High hat and snare.

...then add the snare,

Set the metronome to ♩ = 100

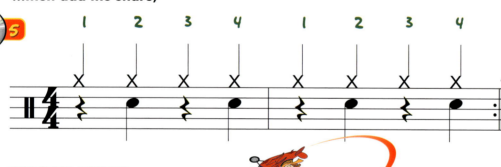

PRACTICE POINTS.

Practice slowly and ensure that you **loop the sequence.**

BRAIN TEASER

High hat, snare and bass drum.

...and finally, the bass drum too!

Set the metronome to ♩ = 100

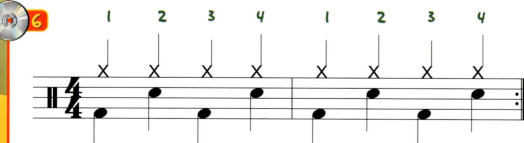

PRACTICE POINTS.

Once you have mastered this sequence try to **up the tempo** and hold a steady speed throughout.

©2008 by Southern Counties Music Services Limited. Photocopying is illegal.

Junior Drum Trainer™ WEEK:4

WEEKLY WORKOUT

Timekeeping and 1/8 notes.

Set the metronome to ♩ = 80

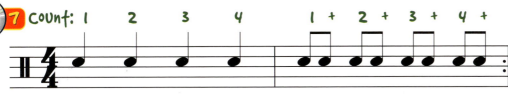

Today, we're looking at **eighth notes**, and how to count them. An eighth note is worth just **half a beat** - twice as fast as a quarter note - count carefully to make sure you stay in time!

TIMEKEEPING means keeping the **tempo** of a piece **STEADY** - it's really important that you're good at this if you're a drummer!
Practising along with a metronome will help you to improve your timekeeping.

HOME TRAINING TIP: Practice your single and double stroke rolls with a metronome.

TRAINING ZONE

New rudiment - the 5 stroke roll.

The **5 stroke roll** is used a lot in classical/orchestral drumming. However, a lot of **Rock** drummers use it to start **Fills** or **Solos**. Notice how the rudiment 'leads' with both hands.

PRACTICE POINTS: Don't pull back before the stroke. Use your wrists and not your arms. Aim for an even sound.

Set the metronome to ♩ = 80

BRAIN TEASER

Your first song - Rock Steady.

The final part of your weekly training session is over the page...so what are you waiting for....?

TURN OVER THE PAGE

Junior Drum Trainer™ WEEK:4 (cont.)

BEAT OUT A SONG

Rock steady.

9
10

Set the metronome to ♩ = 75

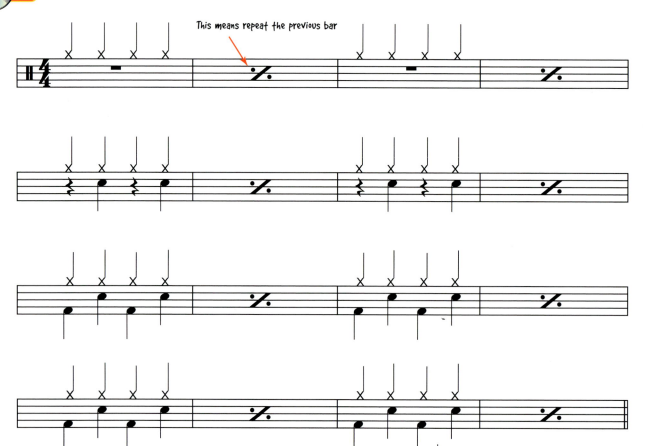

This means repeat the previous bar

Rock Steady finishes with a **crash cymbal.** The notation looks like this ✘
We won't worry about this too much as we don't study these until Book 2.

ROCK 'N' ROLL

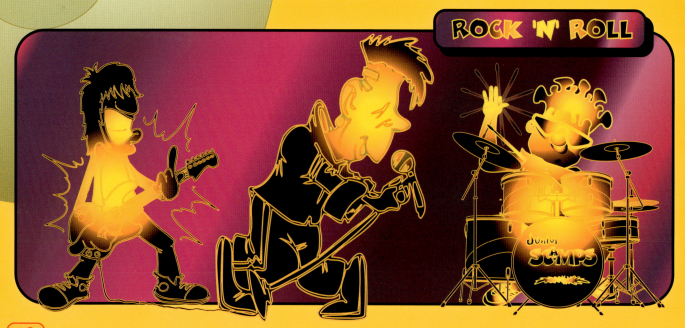

©2008 by Southern Counties Music Services Limited. Photocopying is illegal.

Junior Drum Trainer™ WEEK: 5

WEEKLY WORKOUT

New beat day.

Set the metronome to ♩ = 65

This week we are using **eighth notes** on the high hat. This gives a **quicker feel** to the beat. Just like we did in week two, we will build the beat piece by piece.

Start with just the hi hat.

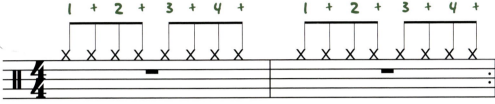

...then add the snare,

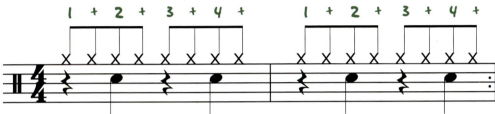

...and finally, the bass drum too!

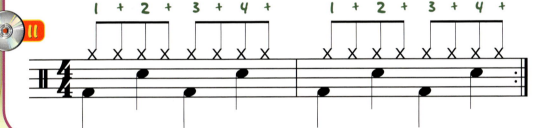

BRAIN TEASER

follow the leader game.

Set the metronome to ♩ = 70

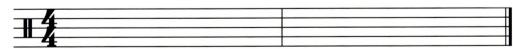

This is a great game to play, and it will help you to develop your **musical ear.**
On the CD, you'll hear **three different rhythms** played on the snare drum, made up of **quarter** and **eighth notes.** We've written out the first one, you've got to work out what the 2nd and 3rd rhythms are and write them in above. Good luck!

©2008 by Southern Counties Music Services Limited. Photocopying is illegal.

Junior Drum Trainer™ WEEK:6

WEEKLY WORKOUT

New rudiment - flams.

Set the metronome to ♩ = 65

Today we're learning to play **Flams**. Set up your sticks above the drum with the right slightly lower than the left. Now drop both together - the **right** should hit **just before** the **left** - that's a flam! Remember to practice both ways round though!

TRAINING ZONE

Counting beats.

Set the metronome to ♩ = 70

Whole note   Half notes   Quarter notes   Eighth notes

We don't just use **quarter** and **eighth notes** - sometimes we need longer notes too! Play the example written above and remember to keep counting!

Once you have mastered it, try playing **Movie Beat** on the next page.

BRAIN TEASER

Drum Reading Race.

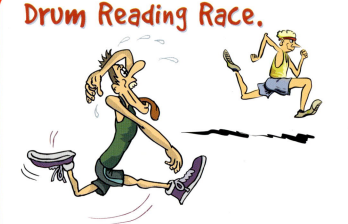

Today we're playing a game to see how quickly you can **recognize the drum voices** on the stave.

Cut out the **Trainer Cards** on page 19 then pass them to a friend to be the quiz master.

See how long it takes to **read 4 cards correctly**, then get training and see if you can beat your time next week!

Week 1: _____ Secs   **Week 2:** _____ Secs

©2008 by Southern Counties Music Services Limited. Photocopying is illegal.

Junior Drum Trainer™ WEEK: 7

15/06

WEEKLY WORKOUT

Double kick day.

16

Set the metronome to ♩ = 70

In this exercise we're playing **eighth notes** on the **bass drum** to speed up your foot work. Try to keep your **right heel up** when playing the **kick!**

TRAINING ZONE

New rudiment - drags.

17

Set the metronome to ♩ = 65

To play a Drag - let the first stick **bounce quickly** on the skin then follow it immediately with a **louder hit** with the other stick.

RR L LL R RR L LL R   RR L LL R RR L LL R

This will take time to master but you will hear a lot of **good drummers** using this technique in fills.

BRAIN TEASER

Fulcrum exercise.

This exercise will help you to **strengthen your grip**. Take your thumb and place it on the end of the stick (butt), then place your index finger under the stick. Keep the rest of your fingers off the stick. NOW - Wiggle it up and down!!

ENDURANCE TEST:
See how long you can wiggle both sticks.

Week 1: ☐ Mins   Week 2: ☐ Mins

14

©2008 by Southern Counties Music Services Limited. Photocopying is illegal.

Junior Drum Trainer™ WEEK:9

WEEKLY WORKOUT

Using rests.

Today we're playing a rhythm with a **combination of different notes and rests**. Try to work out how the rhythm goes! You won't find this example on the CD, you'll have to count carefully to work it out - it's great practice for your **SIGHT READING**.

TRAINING ZONE

Expanding rudiments.

Today we are going to expand some rudiments on the kit.

18 1) Single stroke roll.   Set the metronome to ♩ = 65

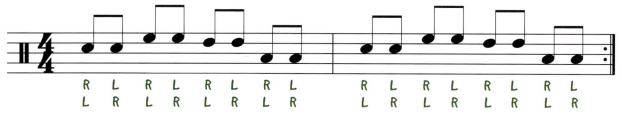

R L R L R L R L   R L R L R L R L
L R L R L R L R   L R L R L R L R

19 2) Flams.   Set the metronome to ♩ = 65

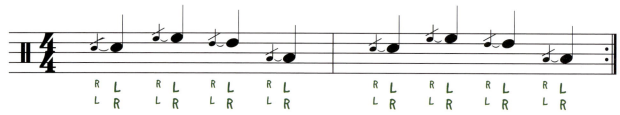

R L R L R L R L   R L R L R L R L
L R L R L R L R   L R L R L R L R

20 3) Paradiddle.   Set the metronome to ♩ = 65

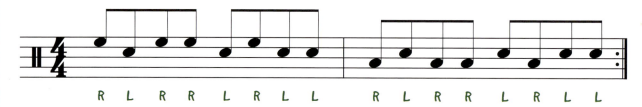

R L R R L R L L   R L R R L R L L

©2008 by Southern Counties Music Services Limited. Photocopying is illegal.

Junior Drum Trainer™ WEEK:10

PUTTING IT ALL TOGETHER

Your first drum fills.

Some fills can be played **leading** with **either hand** - try these first two both ways round.

21 Single stroke fill.   Set the metronome to ♩ = 65

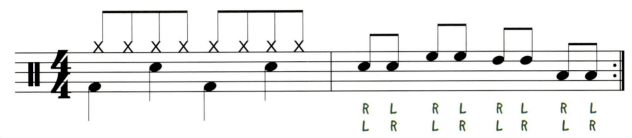

22 Flam fill.   Set the metronome to ♩ = 65

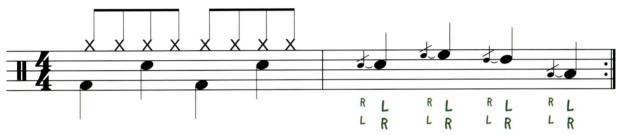

Other fills need to be played a certain way, like these.
If you play a **left handed kit**, you'll need to **swap the sticking** around for these two.

23 Paradiddle fill.   Set the metronome to ♩ = 65

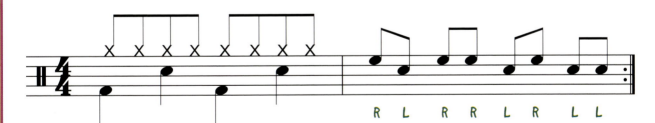

24 Double stroke fill.   Set the metronome to ♩ = 65

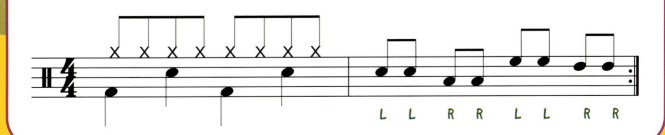

©2008 by Southern Counties Music Services Limited. Photocopying is illegal.

Junior Drum Trainer™ WEEK:10 (cont.)

BEAT OUT A SONG

All together.

Set the metronome to ♩ = 75

We hope you have enjoyed Book 1 and your first 10 weeks of playing the Drums!

To finish off we have composed a piece called **'All together'**. This will use a selection of rudiments learned from this book. Don't forget the 4 beat count in. **Good luck, see you in the next book!**

Junior Drum TRAINER CARDS

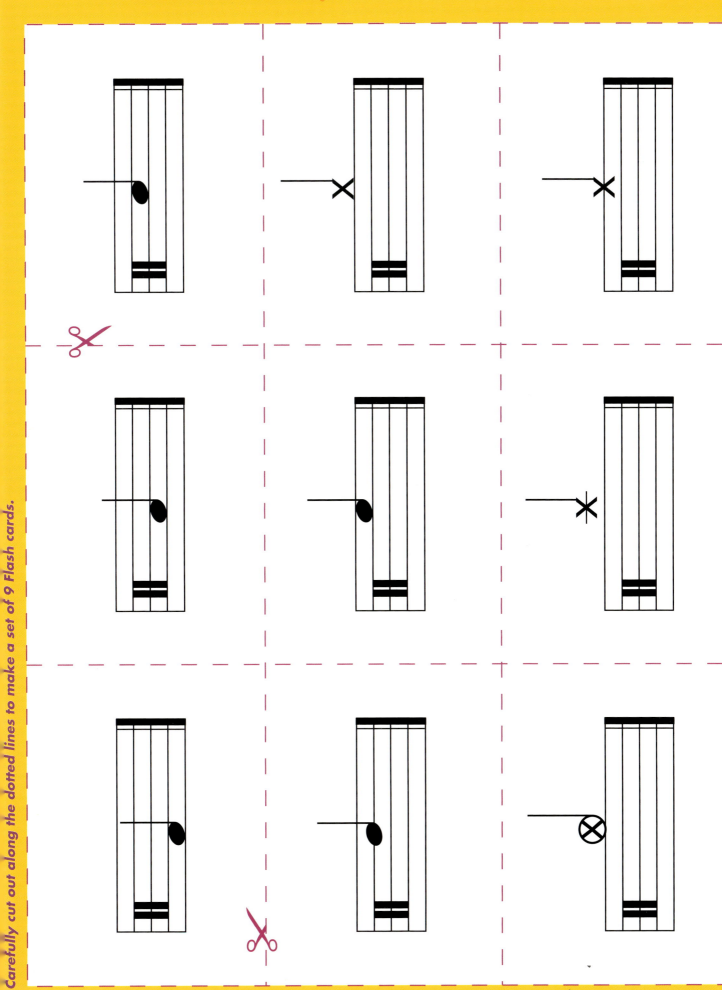

Carefully cut out along the dotted lines to make a set of 9 Flash cards.

©2008 by Southern Counties Music Services Limited. Photocopying is illegal.

Junior Drum TRAINER CARDS

Snare drum	High hat closed	Ride Cymbal
Floor tom	High tom	Crash Cymbal
Kick drum	Medium tom	High hat open

TESTING TIMES

Try the events below to get faster at reading your **TRAINER CARDS**. You can be **"The FASTEST or the STRONGEST!"** The choice is yours.

Best of luck!!

All the running events should be answered **as fast as possible**.

For the field events you must answer all the notes as accurately as possible. If you get one wrong, **stop** and try to complete the challenge **another day**.

TOTALS

EVENT 1	100m Sprint	- Each Correct Answer =	10 metres	secs
EVENT 2	110m Hurdles	- Each Correct Answer =	10 metres	secs
EVENT 3	Javelin	- Each Correct Answer =	10 metres (max 100 metres)	metres
EVENT 4	Hammer	- Each Correct Answer =	10 metres (max 90 metres)	metres
EVENT 5	Shot-put	- Each Correct Answer =	2 metres (max 20 metres)	metres
EVENT 6	Long Jump	- Each Correct Answer =	1 metre (max 9 metres)	metres
EVENT 7	Triple Jump	- Each Correct Answer =	2 metres (max 18 metres)	metres
EVENT 8	Pole Vault	- Each Correct Answer =	1 metre (max 6 metres)	metres
EVENT 9	200m Sprint	- Each Correct Answer =	20 metres	secs
EVENT 10	800 metres	- Each Correct Answer =	100 metres	secs
EVENT 11	1500 metres	- Each Correct Answer =	150 metres	secs
EVENT 12	Marathon	- Each Correct Answer =	1 mile	secs

GRAND TOTAL